Wine 101

Gerald C. Hammon

Illustrations by Jerry Jesurun

Bremo Press
Phoenix, Arizona

Wine 101

Published by
Bremo Press
P.O. Box 30604
Phoenix, AZ 85046-0604

All rights reserved.
Copyright © 1993 by Gerald C. Hammon
No part of this book may be reproduced or transmitted
in any form or by any means, electronic or mechanical
including photocopying, recording, or by any
information storage and retrieval system without
permission in writing from the publisher.

Text illustrations: Jerry Jesurun

Publisher's Cataloguing-In-Publication Data

Hammon, Gerald C.
Wine 101/by Gerald C. Hammon
I. Wine and wine making
641.22   LC 93-74725
ISBN Number: 0-9638058-3-5

Printed in the United States of America

0 9 8 7 6 5 4 3 2 1

For Drayton Swartz,
who is an exceptional wine mentor.

For Ted Fuller,
who encouraged me to keep writing.

And for Shary,
who inspired me to do this project.

CONTENTS

Basics of Wine	1
Learning What You Need To Know	3
An Introduction To Wine Terms	7
Red or White	7
Dry	9
Fruit, Tannin, Oak, Acid	12
Nose, Legs, etc.	15
Wine Labels	20
Corked versus Screw-tops	23
So How Do I Get The Cork Out?	26
Which Wines To Buy?	29
Tasting	30
Alternatives	34
Wine Merchant	34
Restaurants	35
Wine Guides	36
Varietals	39
Cabernet Sauvignon	40
Pinot Noir	42
Zinfandel	44
Merlot	46
Petit Sirah or Syrah	48
Gamay Beaujolais	50
Chardonnay	51
Sauvignon Blanc	53
Gewurztraminer	54
Chenin Blanc	55
Johannesburg Riesling	57
White Zinfandel	59
Generic Wines	60
Varietal Jug Wine	65
Champagne or Sparkling Wine	67
Storing Your Wine	69
Over The Hill Wines	73
Serving Wine	75
Temperature	77
Airing	79
Enjoying	80
A Primer On Wine	81

A Lighthearted Look at the Basics of Wine

Two weeks ago, you were offered the chance of a lifetime! Megabucks, Incorporated, actually offered you a job (and at **four times** the salary you were earning at Poverty, Ltd.). Tonight is your chance to make it or break it. J. Arthur Megabucks and his wife Medusa asked you out to dinner. Never mind that it's dutch treat. This is the moment! You were impressed when they picked you up in their Bentley Salon. You were totally awed when they led you into the dining room at Le Bigbucks Eaterie. But now, J. Arthur is handing you **the wine list!**

All right. So your total experience with wine is the stuff you buy on sale at Food On The Cheap. You aren't even sure of the difference between red and white, let alone Pinot Chardonnay and Petit Syrah. Your career, your future, and as your significant other stares at you, your love life seem to hang in the balance.

What are you going to do?

Take heart!

This book could be
   the key to your future.

   Of course it may get you in such trouble you might not have a future!

   HOWEVER, it is guaranteed to help to lighten those burdensome future days when you are looking for a job.

HOW CAN I EVER LEARN WHAT I NEED TO KNOW ABOUT WINE?

You're standing just inside the door of your favorite liquor store gazing at four solid aisles jammed with bottle after bottle of wine. Some bottles are short and squat, others are tall and tapered, and there is a welter of colors. There are more wineries than you ever knew existed and each seems to produce a dozen types of wine. You pride yourself on being a take-charge person but this is overwhelming. You're feeling intimidated and it's not a good feeling.

One purpose of this book is to help you feel more confident, because intimidation can be a major obstacle to the enjoyment of the nectar of the vine! This book will **NOT** direct you to specific bottles of wine. A number of books on wine do just that. In my experience the wines they recommend are usually gone from the wine merchant's shelves before the books leave the printer! What good does it do you to know that Bazoom Vineyards 1987 Pinot Noir was an absolute knock-out if the only way you can obtain a bottle is to steal it from someone's wine cellar? And no, you cannot necessarily depend on Bazoom Vineyards 1988 Pinot Noir being just as good. So before you become even more confused and intimidated, let's focus on why people drink wine.

The most obvious and simple answer is that people drink wine because they enjoy it. Unfortunately, simple answers aren't always in vogue. People get mixed up with "the right wine for the right food" and the prestige of setting a bottle of Premier Crux French chateaux wine on their table. (Even if you don't know what Premier Crux or French chateaux means, you get the drift that this stuff costs BIG bucks.) Sadly, choosing wine to drink can be intimidating because some wine connoisseurs want it that way.

In fact, one of the biggest problems with the enjoyment of wine may be some of the people who drink it. And we aren't referring to the folks under the railroad overpass slugging down a bottle of white lightning carefully wrapped in a brown paper bag. The ones you have to watch out for are the ones who look at you as if you just crawled out from under the wall panelling when you tell them the White Zinfandel you're drinking is very good. They have a habit of appearing at your elbow, peering critically into your glass and muttering something about, "Did that come in a corked bottle or a bottle with a screw-on top?" or "Pleasant, but pale in comparison to the wonderful Obscurity Vintners 1976 Blush Special Reserve!"

They are typically people who have cultivated an expression reminiscent of a pre-World War II Austrian Duke and a way of rolling French wine names around on the tip of their tongues. They can discourse at nauseating length on the virtues of 1976

French Bordeaux as opposed to 1974 California Cabernet Sauvignon. Actually there's not much chance you'll have the opportunity to try either unless you are planning to study for a Doctorate in Ancient Wines, or your last name is Trump.

Unless you **enjoy** being made to feel inferior, ignore the wine snob. These are people who believe that unless the label reads "Chateau lé Kings Ransom", it isn't worth drinking. Their hierarchy of wine begins with the wine produced from three grape vines hidden away in a remote French village on the Chateau de Mumble Mumble, each bottle of which (there are only twenty-four produced each year) costs $2,038.75 and never descends from that rarified atmosphere to the likes of what you can buy in the supermarket. More importantly, fun and wine are words they never use together.

But wine and fun DO belong together! That's why wine snobs should be left in their own etherial world. Contrary to their every pretention, if it tastes good to you, that's all that matters.

Of course wine offers the opportunity to learn and appreciate new tastes and new experiences if you're willing. But by the same token, there's nothing wrong with the familiar if you enjoy it. The Gallo family made a fortune capitalizing on that concept. They strive to have each bottle of a Gallo varietal* taste like every other bottle of that varietal, and as long as each bottle is good - who can fault them. The French produce won-

---

* Varietal: Wine made from a specific type of grape. More on this later.

derful wine. But they are sensible enough to know they can't drink the exquisite stuff at every meal. (Most of them aren't named Trump.) And so the bottle on the table at most meals is what they call "vin ordinaire". In America, we call it "jug wine". And we're fortunate in that American jug wines are by and large not "ordinaire" but very, very good.

AN INTRODUCTION TO WINE TERMS

Wine terminology can admittedly be dismaying. To drink beer, all you have to know is whether you like "Silver Bullets" or "Bud Light". No one asks you to pronounce tongue twisting French names, or to figure out whether you like red or white (particularly when it seems few wines are either), or understand the complexities of "dry". All you have to do is belly up to the bar and yell, **"Gimme a beer."**

(But beware, there are beer snobs. Fortunately, unless you frequent boutique breweries, you're not likely to meet them.)

You can, if you're so inclined, belly up to the bar and yell, **"Give me a wine!"** But be advised, you will have to answer at least one question, "Red or white?" And you will undoubtedly have to put up with some cheap shots from the boilermaker crowd. Since you bought this book to stop being an object of scorn, let's take some of the mystery out of wine terminology.

Let's begin with

RED OR WHITE?

Color is basic to understanding wine. You were probably taught your colors in Kindergarten (so you thought). We are about to convince you that you didn't attend a "with it" kindergarten. Take **Red** for instance. You know the color red when you see it.

If not, please forgive me for hoping:
a) you live in a town 2000 miles from me,
b) you don't have a driver's license, or
c) you're color-blind.

In wine, you need to add to your color definitions. Red wine for instance can range in color from a deep purple that almost seems black all the way to an insipid pink that looks like someone added too much water to the food coloring.

White on the other hand has little resemblance to the color on your kitchen walls. (After all, you wouldn't be too hep on drinking something that reminded you of Milk of Magnesia.) White wines actually range in color from a pale straw to pink.

There are even wines that split the difference. You'll see them under such names as "Blush" or "Rosé". If you are over 50, you won't have any trouble with the term "blush" because you'll recall that blush once meant the color of an embarrassed person's cheeks. Since no one in the United States has been embarrassed about anything since 1946, this term might need further definition for those of you not studying your Social Security benefits.

So to summarize, wines are characterized as being white, blush or rosé, or red. The range of actual colors is as follows:

White

A wine that is transparent or clear, or a light pink, light straw or even a pale green. (The pale green doesn't look as bad as it sounds.)

Blush

Over 55: make a lewd suggestion to your significant other and watch the color of his/her cheeks.

Under 55: consult Webster's Unabridged Dictionary.

Red

Wine ranging in color from barely ripe strawberries to very ripe plums.

Some hard core wine drinkers claim you can tell whether people drank red or white wine by looking at their teeth. Try it. Look in a mirror after you've sampled some wine. If your teeth are temporarily stained purple, there is a high probability you drank red wine. If your teeth are not stained, it was probably white or blush wine. If you drink too much wine, the headaches can also vary with color. Red Wines tend to create more "interesting" pains than white.

We'll discuss how wine gets its color later. For now, suffice it to say that it doesn't come from the chemist's laboratory (fortunately).

Another term you will encounter early in your wine drinking career is

DRY

Dry wine?

No, it isn't wine produced in the Sahara desert. But you do well to ask.

How can a liquid be dry? Ridiculous.

One day you will be standing in front of row upon row of wine offerings, trying to sort out of all the possible choices which wine will a) not cost an arm and a leg, b) still taste good, and c) not make you look like a complete idiot in front of your company that evening. The wine merchant, who really does not want you to be intimidated and more importantly, wants you to like what you buy will probably ask,

"Do you prefer a dry or sweet wine?"

"SWEET!" you say, envisioning your cheeks sucked inward against your tongue by a liquid that tastes like it came from your Grandmother's medicine cabinet. Well, maybe yes, sweet; then again, maybe no. Wine can be too sweet, particularly when matched with food that isn't flavored with the knock-out punch of two tablespoons of curry or a cup of jalepeño peppers.

Let's end the confusion once and for all. Dryness is a measure of how much sugar is left in the wine after it has fermented. In short, the drier the wine, the less sugar left after fermentation. Dry wine isn't necessarily judged by its "pucker power", nor its ability to substitute for vinegar in your homemade salad dressing.

Scientists have determined that there are only four basic "tastes": salt, sweet, sour and bitter. As you become more familiar with wine and begin looking at wine guides *, you may remember this statement and wonder how, with only salt, sweet, sour and bitter to work with, the writers of the wine guides can come up with descriptions like this:

> *Hints of honey, peaches and butterscotch are nicely balanced by a herbal backdrop. The wine's brief association with oak has left a touch of tannin that balances nicely with the hint of residual sugar.*

Strangely enough, descriptions such as these are not mere hype, nor did the writer choose flavor descriptions at random from his well thumbed Webster's Unabridged. This is an attempt to describe the complex ways those four tastes can meld together in your mouth in a good wine with an impact you'll never find in a brew!

Because sweet is only one of the four basic tastes, winemakers are careful not to let the natural sugar overpower the rest of the ingredients of the wine. We all know people who ladle salt by the cup measure over everything that is set before them. One wonders if they ever taste anything else. So it is with wine. You can stick to wines like Muscatel (most

---

* See section on Wine Guides.

commonly found in subway station staircases after midnight), which are cloyingly sweet if that's your bag.

There are excellent wines that can honestly be termed "sweet". Usually, they have been crafted as desert wines. They are served after a meal or alone. These have little in common with the sweet versions of white lightning that fuel skid row.

Most wine is not "sweet". However, sweetness or dryness is a useful measure of how a wine might fit into your dining plans. I was surprised to learn from a server in a Mexican restaurant that a semi-dry (slightly sweet) White Zinfandel could be an excellent counterpart to a "hot" Mexican meal. The residual sugar offsets the impact of the chili in a way that few other substances can. In addition to standing up to the spiciness of the food, it also serves as a needed "fire extinguisher" if the chili turns out to be more than you bargained for. A truly dry wine would not have the same effect. (You quickly learn in the Southwest that water is no solution for potent chili. You can pour it down and your mouth will still feel like a four alarm fire.)

At the other extreme, a semi-dry wine will do little for your delicately seasoned roast rack of lamb. In time, as you begin to branch out among the many wines offered, you'll begin to gain confidence that a dry wine might indeed be just the right accompaniment for that special dinner.

FRUIT, TANNIN, OAK, ACID

While sugar plays a vital role in how a wine tastes, other ingredients may play an even greater role.

Since wine is made from grapes, it stands to reason the flavor of the grapes will have a decided effect on what the wine tastes like. Unfortunately, going down to the local farmer's market and buying a bunch of grapes isn't likely to tell you very much about wine. Table grapes are grown to be eaten. There have been attempts to make wine out of such grapes as Thompson Seedless, but I understand they didn't go over very well. I love Thompson Seedless in bunches, but doubt if I'd find them attractive bottled. If you happen to have the opportunity to sample wine grapes from the vine, you will probably find them tart and rather unfamiliar in taste. Nevertheless, it is the fruit that provides the basic flavor structure to any wine.

The fruit also contains acid although not the kind you find in batteries. The acid is like that of citrus, balancing the sweetness and providing a certain tang to the taste. The skins and stems of red grapes also provide tannin which gives red wines their astringency. Each can be as important as the sugar and fruit of the grape.

If you read a wine guide, you will note that the fruit in some wines has been overwhelmed by other characteristics. In other words, the taste of the fruit was weak, and the dominant sense one gets is drinking a bottle of liquid oak, or perhaps vinegar. However, when all aspects of the wine are in balance, the final product is greatly enhanced.

Two influences on taste are related directly to the manner in which the wine is aged. Wine can be aged in giant stainless steel tanks, large redwood barrels or even small French oak casks. If the same wine was divided and some aged in the stainless steel tanks and some in the oak casks, they would be quite different by the time they were bottled. The wine in the oak casks would pick up a vanilla-like flavor from the wood. The stainless steel tanks impart no flavor at all but preserve the fruit character of the wine. Redwood barrels give a light "woody" taste, but not vanilla as the oak casks do. The skill of the winemaker is evident in the way in which he or she uses these processes to influence the final product.

The final product is a combination of the flavor of the grapes themselves, the processing of the wine and the method of aging. Of these, the grapes are obviously the most important element. It is the grapes that are the most variable. No manner of processing nor skill of a winemaker can overcome a bad year. The temperatures in the wine growing regions may have been too hot or too cold. It may have rained too much or too little. Worse, it may have rained right at harvest, rotting the grapes on the vine before they could be picked. Early frost may have forced the harvest before the grapes had sweetened enough for a great wine. Given all that can go wrong, it is amazing there is still so much good wine produced each year.

NOSE, LEGS, AND OTHER ODDITIES

I know. Just when you were starting to relax, I jump in with the truly off-the-wall terminology. The more scholarly inclined among you may be wondering about this sudden anthropomorphic approach to wine. The rest of you are staring at your wine glass and wondering if I'm some kind of weirdo.

NOSE

Remember the dinner with J. Arthur Megabucks when you found yourself sitting in Le Bigbucks Eaterie with the wine list in hand? Having survived the selection process with the judicious assistance of the server, you remembered there was a ritual to serving wine. Fortunately, at that moment, you happened to glance across at the adjacent table where a bottle of wine was being delivered by the wine steward. The steward showed the guy who had ordered the wine the label. O.K. Makes sense. Did the wine steward get the right bottle? Nothing like finding out you ordered a moderately priced bottle of wine and were served AND BILLED for the stuff that pays for the restaurant owner's daughter's education. Then there was the business about the cork. Once the cork was removed, the wine steward offered the cork to the man and he put it to his nose and smelled it.

All right. No problem. I've done that before. But what exactly am I smelling the cork for? Why is this part of the ritual?

Smelling the cork allows a first sample of the aroma of the wine. In older European wine cellars, the high humidity meant that wine labels were often so mouldy that they couldn't be read. In those instances, the winemaker's label on the cork was one guarantee that you were actually drinking what you paid for. Fortunately, unless your restaurant has its wine shipped directly from the Panamanian rain forest to the table, you probably won't have to worry about relying on the cork to know what you are drinking. In most instances, ==smelling the cork allows you to sample the aroma of the wine and determine at the same time if the bottle is in good condition.==

If it's not, any reputable restaurant will take the bottle back and replace it with another. Wine can be kept too long, or under poor conditions, and instead of a delight, you end up drinking a fright. If you are home, and the wine smells like plums that have been in the sun too long, I offer you the advice of a dear friend and wine lover who says that you should immediately consign that bottle to you basic salad dressing ingredients.

The next step in the ritual came as the steward poured a tiny amount in a glass and handed it to the one who had ordered the wine. You watched remembering that in a short time **YOU** would have to repeat this performance. The diner swirled the wine in the glass, looked at it as if determining whether or not a fly had landed therein and then stuck his nose in the glass.

Nose. No, not the beak on the

chap with the wine glass in hand. Wine has a nose, or more accurately, wine gives off odors. If it is good wine, it usually will smell good. In fact, one of the true enjoyments of wine is its fragrance. Researchers report the nose can distinguish 16,000 different smells (not all of which we want to be reminded of). Expensive bourbon may be smooth, but we don't spend much time talking about its smell. With wine, smell is part of the enjoyment.

Swirling the wine in the glass helps free the ingredients in the wine that gives it its nose. (Nose is actually a much more pleasant term than odor - particularly if you can't help but think of odor in terms of **B.O.** - body odor of the unwashed to those who don't remember ancient Lifebuoy Soap radio ads. And fragrance, while a correct term, may be a bit much for male readers who are striving to maintain their macho image.) It is helpful if the wine is in the right kind of glass, but we'll talk about that later.

Some wine actually smells better than it tastes. And there are delightful tasting wines that have little nose. Winemakers strive to develop wines that have both, thus increasing the over-all enjoyment of their product. Actually, as those white gowned actors with stethoscopes around their necks on late night T.V. tell us, taste and smell work together. Real doctors tell us the same thing, but who listens to them. So a wine with a good nose has a better chance of also tasting delicious.

LEGS?

You want your wine to have something to stand on, don't you?

Wait. Wait!! Before you return this book for a refund and reduce me again to poverty, allow me to explain.

Legs is the term used by wine drinkers to describe what happens (or doesn't happen) when the wine is swirled about the glass. If when you quit swirling, the wine takes it's own sweet time returning to the bottom of the glass, leaving little tracks or streams on the upper portion of the glass, it is said to have legs. It's a sign the wine has body. (Body? Legs? Nose?) Well, it's better than having no body. Ask any neighborhood ghost.

In all honesty, legs will never do for you what nose will. But it is another test that the wine you are about to drink is worth what you paid for it. Wine that lacks body tends to be insipid, limp, watery. Of course the wine should not have so much body that you wonder if it is beginning to congeal.

CLARITY

Clarity and color work together. Take a glass of wine and hold it up to the light. Obviously, it should not have little creepy crawly things swimming around in it. (If it does, forget even the salad dressing approach.) It shouldn't be murky. The appearance of a glass of good wine should remind you of the look of an exquisite pane of stained glass. Ideally it will have a ==brilliance== to it. It should at least be ==clear.== Wine that looks like coffee with a bit of creme stirred in would have little visual appeal, and probably not much taste appeal.

WINE LABELS

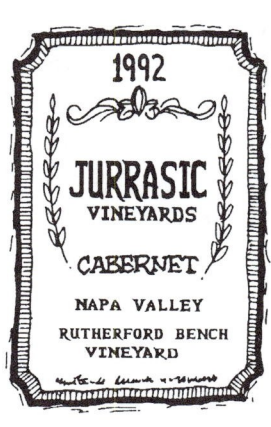

American wines are surprisingly straightforward in their labeling, particularly when you compare them with French wine labels. The producer's name is usually prominent, which when you first start buying wine is of little help. After all, if you don't know anything about wineries, it doesn't help to know which winery made this bottle. But when you discover a particular winery seems to have a flair for putting out wine that you like, you'll appreciate the prominence of the name of the producer (particularly when you are sorting through 26 different Cabernet Sauvignons looking for "your" winery.)

If the wine is a varietal, and most are, the varietal name (name of the grape the wine was made from) is also prominent. Be grateful American wineries do it this way. The French label their wine by region and sometimes only by producer.

Finally, the most important information of all (except the price tag!) is the vintage. Vintage is the year in which the grapes were picked. Wines from the same vines and the same wineries can vary infinitely from year to year. 1990 may have been a stand-out year for many red wines. 1989 was not. If you walked into a liquor store looking for Bilgewater 1990 Cabernet Sauvignon on a friend's recommendation as a great wine, you might be sadly disappointed if you took home a bottle of Bilgewater's 1989 Cabernet instead. Great wines do tend to disappear rapidly from wine merchant's shelves. Poor wines hang around until clearance sales.

The variables in wine making are complex: weather, soil, skill of the vineyardist (the one who tends the vineyard) and vintner (the one who makes the wine). And all of these can change. It can rain during the harvest, or not rain at all that year. The skilled wine maker who produced the knockout 1988 and 1989 wines may have retired. The weather may never have warmed up enough to bring the sugar content of the grapes to the ideal level, or it may have gone up too fast and for too long. So vintage is important.

The label may contain a vineyard designation meaning that 75 percent or more of the grapes came from that single vineyard. In some cases, this is pure and simple snob appeal. However, some vineyards are known for the quality of their grapes, and wines from those vineyards have a better chance of being quality wines than those from more general locations. They also tend to cost more.

Wines that don't contain a vineyard label often are labeled with the county, region or state in which the grapes were grown. County labels can be instructive when you come to know something of the wine growing regions of that particular state. For instance, most wine drinkers are familiar with Napa county in California as a wine paradise and would expect wine with a Napa label to be worth buying. A California wine purchaser might be more reserved about buying a wine with a San Joaquin or Fresno county label (in California's hot central valleys), even though a sizeable portion of the state's bulk wine and table grape production is located there, because the area is not noted for producing outstanding wines.

For a long time, people thought that only certain limited areas (the Napa Valley in California; New York's Finger Lakes region) were capable of producing good wine. Today, there is hardly a state in the union that doesn't have at least one winery, and regions once thought devoid of appeal are producing excellent wines. So even though it's instructive to know where the wine came from, it may not be all that helpful in discriminating between one bottle and another.

I've purposefully limited the scope of this book to American wines since I didn't want to publish it in four volumes. However, with the notable exception of France, the wines of other countries tend to follow the American pattern of labeling. Even some French export wines are beginning to appear with labels that read as do labels on domestic wines.

CORKED WINE VERSUS SCREW-TOPS

A good definition of frustration is to purchase a bottle of wine, bring it to the table or picnic blanket and found you don't have a cork-screw. Maybe your kids used it to pry the lids off old paint cans. In that moment, you can't help but wonder why most wines are corked. I mean, what are you supposed to do? Bash the neck of the bottle on the edge of the kitchen counter and hope you don't spill too much? Leave dinner cooling on the table (and your significant other heating up at your side - particularly if **they** prepared the meal) while you race down to your local, or not so local convenience store in the vain hope they stock corkscrews. And when you find they don't, do you give up and pick up a bottle with a screw top, vowing never again to fall afoul of a dumb cork?

If you've looked at wine prices, you've undoubtedly noted wine in bottles with screw top lids is less expensive than the corked stuff. In many cases, **considerably** less. So why bother with corks?

Tradition! Besides, just **try** to serve the likes of J. Arthur Megabucks wine from a screwtop bottle! Corks are believed by many to breathe. I know, here we go with this anthropomorphic crap again. Although some reputable wine experts admit a screw top may actually be better in keeping impurities out, there is a firm prejudice that wine will not age in a screw top bottle. And aging is important to many if not most wines. (Actually, the real reason wine bottled with a screw top doesn't age is that it isn't made to age).

Perhaps an explanation is in order. Aging is not generally a term that calls to mind pleasant thoughts. Too often the mind flips immediately through that great card file in the left lobe toward the "A"'s as in arthritis, then to the "S"'s as in senility and so on, ending up inevitably in the "D"'s stuck on the word Death. But be of good cheer. (If that's possible after I've called to mind images of nursing homes and medicare forms.) Some wines **NEED** to age. Don't you wish YOU needed to age. Trust me; there are wines that actually **IMPROVE** with age.

Now this shouldn't be taken to extremes. A bottle from Pharaoh Ramses XII's private wine cellar might have extraordinary historical significance. But I can almost guarantee

that if there was any liquid left in that bottle, cask or whatever, it would definitely **NOT** be a liquid you would want to put in your mouth. Like humans, even the best of wine can age until it is

OVER THE HILL.*

But for the most part, if you are like me, there is more danger of your committing infanticide on a bottle of wine by drinking it too early than allowing it go over the hill.

* See Section on Geriatric Wines

The key thing you need to know is that ==wine which will improve with age is corked.== If J. Arthur Megabucks thinks his premium wines must be corked, no wine maker with his eye on the bottom line is going to bother with screw tops. Now if your wine is meant for immediate consumption and J. Arthur is not among the dinner guests, it will make little difference whether you uncork it or unscrew it.

SO HOW DO I GET THE CORK OUT?

I would not recommend either a) breaking the bottle at the neck or b) those little knife-like gadgets the waiters use. I've never tested how well corks burn, so I also would hesitate to recommend a blow torch.

Those little jackknife gadgets you see in restaurants obviously work as thousands of waiters and waitresses can testify. But they aren't easy to use. If you don't believe that, study the expressions on the face of novice servers as they struggle to manipulate the twisted wire into the cork and then get the complete cork out. It can range from frustration to agony to sheer joy as the cork finally comes free, or to utter defeat when the cork breaks with half still in the bottle.

There are many ways to remove a cork ranging from inexpensive "Ah So's" to flowery brass contraptions on ornamental stands. They all work *most of the time*. The brass contraptions are advertized as able to extract the cork in one turn of the crank and they do work well. It's just that whenever I've had a spare $100 lying around, I had better uses for it (like paying off my super inflated Visa bills - or buying some decent wine and ignoring my super inflated Visa bills as usual) to ever try one of these products. (Actually, I waited until I received one as a present from someone who loved me enough to spend their money on it.)

There are gizmos consisting of a thin hollow needle with a pump which force the cork out through the build-up of air pressure inside the bottle. I can attest to the fact that they work most of the time and they do not turn your wine into cheap bubbly. Sometimes I do wonder if the bottle isn't going to explode before the cork comes out. My personal experience has been that these work better on red wines than white, although I'm at a loss to explain why.

The most common cork pullers are designed so that you screw a twisted wire into the cork and then either by use of a turn screw or flip up handles, you force the body of the cork puller down on the lip of the bottle and extract the cork. Most of these work quite well. They do have an occasional tendency to crumble the cork as the wire passes through. It's a particular problem with some inexpensive wines where the corks tend to be inferior. (Hopefully the wine isn't.) This can leave a residue of cork crumbs as seasoning for your first few glasses. It is a distinct distraction when sampling the wine for clarity. And chewy wine has never been on anyone's "must taste" list. Maybe I should quit buying such cheap wines.

My personal favorite is a device known as the "Ah So". It consists of two thin, curved tines of metal facing each other on a handle. The metal tines are flexible. By rocking the handle back and forth, you will work the tines down between the cork and the neck of the bottle. The "Ah So" is designed so that once you have worked the tines down as far as you can, there is enough pressure on the tines and the cork that when you begin pulling up on the handle, the cork comes too. Works like a charm. And it has yet to leave crumbs of cork in the glass (even when uncorking those $2.98 bottles of middle European wine whose corks define the term "inferior").

In years gone by winemakers took as much pride in their corks as they took in their wines. That was before they were bought out by General Prodigious Amalgamated Leveraged Buyout Corporation. Before long, the accountants took over and came to the seemingly logical conclusion that a cork is a cork is a cork. And they proceeded to buy corks made out of Presto logs. And wine drinkers discovered the joys of straining their wines before drinking.

Actually most wines today come with corks that will at least hold together until it is extracted from the neck of the bottle (unless the wine was made in Rumania before the collapse of communism). And any of the cork pullers you find on the market will no doubt serve you well. The "Ah So's" I referred to shouldn't set you back by more than a few bucks, so don't be tempted to pick up the "Gee Whiz Bang Cork Extractor" in the novelty shop for $39.95. It may not even work as well, and for the difference, you can probably pick up a couple of bottles of very nice wine.

O.K. O.K. BUT HOW DO I LEARN ABOUT WHICH WINES TO BUY?

My liquor store has over thirty brands of wine and I haven't even counted the types. What am I supposed to do? Go out and buy one each? By the time I got done, I'd be so schnockered, I'd never remember what any of them tasted like.

Let's start with one simple caution. Wine is an alcoholic beverage. But it is definitely not the beverage of choice to get blitzed on. To paraphrase Robert Benchley, whiskey is quicker. But we digress. If that was your sole interest, you wouldn't have bought this book, or I should have added a chapter on "Thunderbird, Night Train Express and other cheap paths to oblivion."

Having stated that caution, I can now inform you that, depending on where you live, there is a way you can learn about wines. It is inexpensive, educational, and for most people, downright enjoyable. It's called

WINERY TOURS.

If you live in or near California, consider yourself fortunate indeed (unless you have an aversion to the ground periodically shaking under your feet). California wineries are like the Mecca and Medina of wine lovers - surpassed only slightly by French Chateaux for those fortunate enough to get to Europe periodically. Coastal California from the Los Angeles basin to the northern Redwoods is one vast conglomeration of wineries. They range in size from mom and pop operations who sell their limited production only at the winery to giants who market EVERYWHERE. Most offer tours, and even more importantly,

TASTING

As unbelievable as it sounds, many wineries will take bottles of their current production that they sell for as much as $20 a pop and will let you sample them. While some wineries charge a modest fee for their sampling, at many others it's free! There's no hidden motive. The wineries understand that the best way to get you to buy their product is to allow you to try their wines and see if you like them. There's no high pressure. No ham fisted bruiser nick-named "Meats" removes your car keys and refuses to give them back until you walk out with a case of wine under each arm.

You can sip in silence, commune with your significant other, or partake of the second benefit of a winery's tasting room - the knowledgeable folks who work there. My wife and I still remember tasting wine in a winery that has since become a major presence on liquor store and grocery shelves, and finding out that the elderly man with the twinkle in his eyes and the love of the product who was serving us owned the whole shebang! And it was no small presence in the wine industry even then. Not every wine tasting room is staffed by the owner and his/her family, but most likely, the folks there will not only know about their own wine, they'll know about the neighboring wineries as well.

Ah, but what if I don't like it?

The folks in the tasting room won't care. They will happily provide receptacles for you to pour out anything that sets your teeth ajar. You can even spit it out if the wine you're sampling declares war on your taste buds. There's no embarrassment involved. They'd far prefer you spend time on the wines you do find enjoyable than waste time (and alcohol consumption) on wines you'd never buy.

I can write volumes on "dry" and "nose" and the like. But a knowledgeable winery employee can bring these terms to life as they instruct you on how to enjoy their wine.

If I may, I should offer a personal word of advice. Some folks head for the wine country for a day, determined they are going to sample every wine at every winery in Napa County. You can't do it, and if you try, the only thing you will remember about the day was the Driving Under the Influence conviction and the year you spent without a driver's license.

When starting out, pick two or three of the larger wineries. Go on at least one tour; it's worth it and you'll gain a new appreciation of the complexities of making wine. Then let the hosts in the tasting room guide you through the wines they offer that day. Normally, they begin with white wines, progressing through blush and red and ending with any dessert (sweet) wines they are pouring. They do the tasting in this order because if you start out tasting a block-buster Zinfandel (a red varietal), you'll never appreciate the nuances of the winery's

Sauvignon Blanc (a white). White wines tend to be reserved and subtle. Reds are more assertive. And once you've tasted the desert wine (possibly a Johannesburg Riesling or even a Port), your taste buds simply won't react to the complexities of a good Chardonnay.

After you gain some confidence and begin to discover particular wines you like, try going to smaller wineries. Many are a delightful experience. You may find yourself sampling wine with the actual winemaker over the top of wine barrels currently in use. There won't be the variety, but you won't be disappointed at the quality.

A couple of "insider" tips about wine tasting:

• Try not to go on a weekend. If you must, expect the larger wineries to be crowded. And when the tasting rooms are packed, it's hard for the hosts and hostesses to do much more than simply pour and wash glasses as fast as they can.

• Try lesser known wine areas. California's Napa valley is renown for outstanding wines, but there are excellent wines produced all over California and in several other states. Unfortunately, even on a weekday, highway 29 through the Napa valley can resemble a parking lot on sale day at the shopping mall.

- Be reasonable about how much wine you can consume and still enjoy yourself. You don't **HAVE** to sample every wine offered. And remember, you can pour out what you don't want to drink. Wine tasting rooms are not places for a cheap drunk. We're fortunate wineries put up with the crowds and the abusers and still afford us the opportunity to go and taste.

- AAA puts out an excellent guide to California wineries. Their Tour Books for other states frequently includes information on wineries, including whether tasting or tours are offered and when they are open.

- If you live far from California, don't despair. There's hardly a state in the union (other than the state of anarchy) that doesn't boast at least one winery. New York, Washington, and Oregon all have well developed wine industries. The number of wineries is growing in many other states as well. While California wines have a well deserved reputation for excellence, wines from other states can also be outstanding. They may be cheaper too.

ALTERNATIVES TO THE TASTING ROOMS

YOUR LOCAL WINE MERCHANT

If wineries aren't convenient, and perhaps even if they are, many local wine merchants are offering an inexpensive alternative to adding miles to your family wheels. In addition to selling wine, they offer tasting of a certain number of their wines for a fee. You are afforded an opportunity to taste the offerings of several wineries at one location. This is particularly useful if you are interested in tasting one varietal such as Pinot Noir. Wineries that produce Pinot Noir would usually have only one vintage available or at the most, two. By tasting at your friendly wine merchant's location, you can line up five or six Pinot Noirs and try them all.

Some wine merchants are going a step further and offering tastings at which representatives of wineries are present to discuss their wines. This is an opportunity to both try many different wines and learn about the processes that went into the production of the wine. Alternatively, wine experts may be featured such as food and wine columnists, editors of wine guides or professors of viticulture. They will discuss their impressions of the wineries and the offerings of the evening. The fee for such evenings is generally quite reasonable for what is offered and may include crackers and cheese or other appetizers in addition to the wine samples.

If you live in a state where the only wine merchant is the state liquor store, you might look at the next option.

YOUR FRIENDLY LOCAL EATERIE

While you are guaranteed not to find this added service at BURGERWORLD, you may well find that on occasions when you are venturing out for something more than a pizza, the menus of a few restaurants will actually suggest a specific wine to go with a particular entree. In other restaurants, your server or wine steward would be happy to offer recommendations. Being of a somewhat skeptical bent, I used to think the recommendation would inevitably be for the most expensive wine the restaurant carried. My reasoning told me NO one would actually recommend an inexpensive but drinkable bottle. Besides, if most customers were like me (*CHEAP*), who would buy all those horribly expensive bottles the restaurant had in their inventory.

I've since realized that even if restaurants are unabashedly profit motivated, their satisfaction fortunately comes from presenting meals where food and wine compliment each other. Thus the wine recommended is likely to be an excellent complement for that particular dish and the price is based on the cost of the wine to the owner.

Unfortunately, the restaurant suggestions aren't of much help if there are four people dining and all four are ordering entrees that are polar opposites. In that case, the only suggestion that can be made is a quick trip to the local bookstore with attention given to books on the art of compromise.

Following the restaurant suggestions will introduce you to both new wines and new food-wine matches without forcing you to go through the agony of randomly selecting bottles of wine for your special Chicken South Sea Islands and hoping against hope the wine won't set your guests' teeth ajar. (Besides, the random selection process is Expensive!)

WINE GUIDES

No. We aren't referring to some chap decked out like the little old winemaker of some small Italian village who will guide you through the snares and pitfalls of your local liquor store. But you may have noted that some stores put small write-ups below the shelves where certain wines are stocked. This may say that someone whose name you don't recognize has rated this particular wine 88 points out of 100 or three stars out of four. There will usually be some very laudatory phrases included about the wine.

These are excerpts from wine guides. Wine guides are published journals, obtained for the most part on a subscription basis, in which one or more experts tells you their opinion on various wines. Needless to say, the stores don't post the opinions that read something like this:

The nose shows a wet cardboard character with little fruit. There are dank notes in the finish. You'd best forget this one!

However, you **do** want to know if the wine you are thinking of buying DESERVED that kind of write-up.

And that is how writers of wine guides obtain subscribers. It is almost as important to know which wines the guides report as **BOMBS** as it is to know the ones that blew the wine expert's socks off. You've already discovered wine isn't cheap - particularly good wine. So the last thing you want to do is spend your hard earned money on something that tastes like it was aged in a Mack truck's gas tank.

By the same token, if you have a limited budget (and who doesn't) and don't want to waste your money on insipid, modestly made yet overpriced wine, the guides can be of help. Among the practical information furnished by most guides is the average price paid for the wine. You can then equate ratings to your pocket book and narrow down the choices considerably.

While I am a subscriber to wine guides, I would be the first to admit they are not a substitute for your own tastes. The wine guides make available to you the expertise of people who have put a lot of time into researching wines, new releases, winery procedures and the like which will never hurt you in your quest for good wine. But a wine expert is bound by personal preferences in taste, and if those preferences don't match yours, their opinion should not sway you.

LEARNING WHAT YOU LIKE

All the wine guides and friends' recommendations in the world won't substitute for your own taste. In a way, it's like sex. You can read about it, talk about it, and even see it in "X" rated movies or deodorant commercials, but until you experience it, you will never fully understand what all the uproar is about. In the final analysis, you have to find out what you enjoy through direct experience. In short, you have to try it to find out if you like it.

VARIETALS

A varietal wine is made from a specific grape. The winemaker may add small amounts of other varietals to enhance certain qualities of the wine, but if a wine is called a Zinfandel, you have a right to expect it to be made predominately from Zinfandel grapes. In general, a wine must be made from at least 75% grapes of a specific variety to be termed a varietal wine.

So why would you care?

As you develop experience in trying different varietal wines, you will find that each varietal has certain qualities of taste, bouquet* and appearance that are different from others. And because of those differences, one varietal wine may be much better in a certain setting than another.

This section, which is by no means all inclusive, will try to assist you by describing certain varietal wines. As you read these descriptions, bear in mind that taste is a most subjective experience, and you may find wines to be quite different in taste than someone else has.

---

* Bouquet is the description of the nose (fragrance) a specific varietal should have. It is one of the identifying features (along with taste) of a varietal wine. In other words, a varietal wine should smell a certain way. (just as a cooking sirloin should smell like steak, not salmon.)

CABERNET SAUVIGNON

Grape: Cabernet Sauvignon
Color: Deep Red
Cost: Can be quite expensive
Aging: Most Cabernets improve with aging. Better Cabernets can improve for 20 years.
Food: Lamb, Beef
Dryness: Usually very dry.

Many wine drinkers believe Cabernet Sauvignon to be the Cadillac, or perhaps the Rolls Royce, of wines. (I purposely ignored Lexus since it would seem more appropriate to compare Lexus to Sake!) Cabernet Sauvignon is a deep red wine known for its aging potential and the complexity of its taste. It's not uncommon to see good or merely pretentious Cabernet's selling for up to $50 a bottle. Depending on the bottle, it can enhance most red meats and perhaps some veal or poultry, but would probably be wasted with your teriaki hamburger. One school of thought holds that Cabernet is the perfect companion for lamb. Actually, a good Cabernet would probably complement any meal (with the possible exception of breakfast cereal or a peanut butter and jelly sandwich).

Most wine drinkers remember their first experience with good well aged Cabernet. It's an experience every wine lover should have. Unfortunately, you can't go down to the supermarket, pick up a bottle of Cabernet, open it that evening and expect to have one of wine drinking's great experiences. Some bottles are drinkable when you buy them, but the better Cabernets will improve vastly with aging*.

---

* Stores specializing in wine may age a small selection of wine, but you will pay for the service. We stopped at a favorite Napa Valley winery a while back and priced wine we had bought several years before and were holding. The prices were approaching $100 a bottle for wine they had stored and were now selling. The most cost effective way to enjoy good well aged Cabernet is to buy it when the wine is first offered for sale and store it yourself. Patience is a virtue with good red wine.

PINOT NOIR

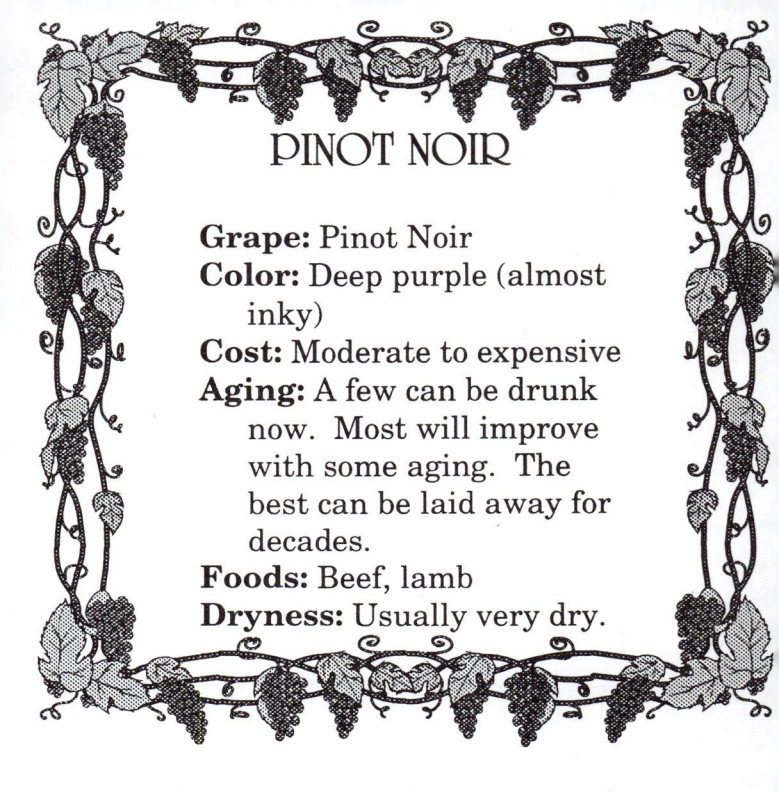

Grape: Pinot Noir
Color: Deep purple (almost inky)
Cost: Moderate to expensive
Aging: A few can be drunk now. Most will improve with some aging. The best can be laid away for decades.
Foods: Beef, lamb
Dryness: Usually very dry.

Pinot Noir was the nemesis of many California vintners and may well have been the red wine that established Oregon's and Washington's reputation as prime producers of good grapes. Not that every California Pinot Noir is terrible and every north coast Pinot Noir excellent. Many California Pinot Noirs are very good. However, Pinot Noir seems to be a grape that is very particular about where it is grown. The French use the Pinot Noir grape as the basis of their outstanding wines from Burgundy.

Whereas Cabernet is said to be a good wine for lamb, Pinot Noir is similarly touted for beef. There are those who say this is the wine to have if the main course is a steak. I won't disagree although I've enjoyed steak with Zinfandel, Cabernet, Petite Syrah and even H_2O. Depending on the style, Pinot Noir might complement anything from a highly spiced meat dish to veal. Pinot Noir can benefit from aging, and some will be drinkable for your grandson's baptism even if you buy it when you get married.

As wineries gain experience, superb Pinot Noirs are coming on the market. Fortunately, the pricing hasn't caught up to the Cabernets and you can buy an outstanding Pinot Noir for quite a bit less than top rated Cabernets. And Pinot Noir can be every bit as complex and rewarding.

ZINFANDEL

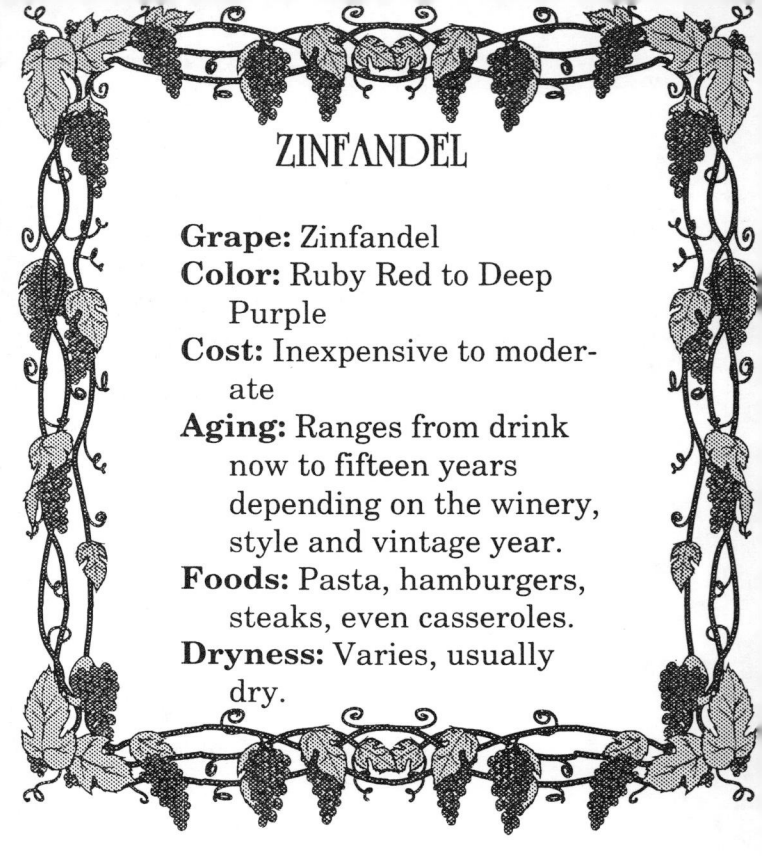

Grape: Zinfandel
Color: Ruby Red to Deep Purple
Cost: Inexpensive to moderate
Aging: Ranges from drink now to fifteen years depending on the winery, style and vintage year.
Foods: Pasta, hamburgers, steaks, even casseroles.
Dryness: Varies, usually dry.

Zinfandel is my personal favorite among the red wines. It is an extremely versatile wine that can be made in a truly amazing number of styles ranging from robust, high alcohol blockbusters to exquisitely balanced complex wines that make you wonder why you waste your money on Cabernet. Although Zinfandel usually does not require as much aging as Cabernet, I still have some Zinfandel that a wine guide recommended holding for ten years before drinking. Other Zin's are the type you can buy, take home, open, serve with your pasta and not be disappointed.

While there are variations in all varietals depending on where the grapes were grown and in what year, Zinfandel tends to be among the most diverse. This can be a problem when you discover a particular Zin you like, only to find that the following year, the Zinfandel from the same winemaker tastes entirely different. It can also be a problem if you have particular expectations about

Zinfandel based on always buying from a winemaker in the Napa Valley, and then try a bottle made by a vintner in the foothills of the Sierra Nevada mountains. Both are Zinfandels but they may be amazingly different. That, to me, is part of the fun of Zinfandel.

Because there are such wide variations in Zinfandel wines, Zinfandel will go with a great variety of foods ranging from the simple to the complex: pasta to Tornados of Beef. Whereas top quality Cabernets cost enough to make you wonder if you should drink it or frame it, Zinfandel is usually affordable. And that means you can experiment without being overly fearful of the consequences.

MERLOT

Grape: Merlot
Color: Dark Red
Cost: Moderate
Aging: Many Merlots can be drunk now; most will improve with a year or more of aging.
Foods: Merlot will complement veal, lamb, beef and some fowl.
Dryness: Usually very dry.

Merlot traditionally was used as a blending wine to temper the rough edges of Cabernet Sauvignon. The French always knew you could make a good wine out of Merlot, but Americans took a long time to discover what the French had known for centuries. It's price won't give you apoplexy and it shares many similarities in taste with Cabernet.

A few years back, you would have had to look long and hard to find Merlot on the wine shelves of your local wine merchant. Now there are a growing number of wineries that are producing Merlot for something other than a blending agent. Wine drinkers are richer for this new option in the world of reds. As a new varietal wine in America, Merlot is produced in a variety of styles. Increasingly, Merlot is produced as a wine with definite aging potential. The best guide to aging potential and length of aging will be either the producer or your local wine merchant.

Like the other red wines, Merlot can complement most red meats. Most

Merlots have the body and the complexity to stand up to the heavier pastas and depending on the style might go well with certain poultry dishes.

PETITE SIRAH OR SYRAH

Grape: Durif
Color: Intense purple
Cost: Moderate to expensive
Aging: 1 to 10 years; some longer
Foods: Barbecued steaks, seasoned pastas, highly spiced dishes.
Dryness: Generally very dry.

 Petite Sirah is not a wine that is commonly available. A few wineries produce it and it does happen to be a personal favorite. It's easy to confuse Petite Sirah with Syrah, a similar dark red wine. Some wineries bottle their Petite Sirah under the Syrah name, even though there is only a minimal amount of true Syrah bottled in the United States. While not identical, both Petite Sirah and Syrah tend to be big inky tannic wines.

 Petite Sirah is a wine that will literally color your tongue and teeth, so don't drink it before heading out to J. Arthur Megabucks' employees reception - particularly if J. Arthur Megabucks' wife Medusa is a member of the Womens' Christian Temperance Union!

 Petite Sirah can be one of those reds that will tend to call attention to itself instead of what you're serving, so it is not a wine for all occasions. It can also be rough and tannic if not well aged; and indeed, some Sirahs probably will not smooth out for the next century. It lacks some of the complexity of Cabernets and Pinot Noirs, but when you encounter a robust Sirah that has its fruit, tannin and oak in balance, you won't forget the experience. Sirah will complement red meats and if it is a true blockbuster, it will go with that special recipe that takes in half of your spice rack. Sirah will overwhelm mild or delicate foods so save it for your special spaghetti, or as a different companion to a good steak.

GAMAY BEAUJOLAIS

Grape: Gamay
Color: Rich purple
Cost: Inexpensive to moderate
Aging: Drink now!
Foods: Veal, lamb, cheese
Dryness: Semi-dry (in other words, little pucker power).

    Gamay Beaujolais is the object of an annual French celebration, in which the new wine is tasted and feted depending on how the vintage turned out. It is a light, drinkable red wine that is not meant to spend any time at all in a wine cellar. This is definitely the wine you can pick up at the store, open that night and be eminently satisfied.

    This is <u>not</u> the wine to stand up to your rich cream sauces or your heavily spiced meat dishes. But I have had a wonderful food experience with a well made Gamay and roast leg of lamb.

    It used to be that most of the Gamay's you saw on the wine shelves were from France, but now some American wineries are starting to produce good Gamay's. They can vary greatly from year to year, so this is another one of those wines that if you liked it last year - you may not this year.

CHARDONNAY

Grape: Pinot Chardonnay
Color: Pale straw
Cost: Moderate to expensive
Aging: Many Chardonnays benefit from aging. Some may be aged for 5 to 10 years and improve in quality. Others may be drunk soon after purchase.
Foods: Fish, poultry, veal.
Dryness: Dry

Most winemakers have dropped the Pinot from their bottles and label them simply Chardonnay. If Cabernet Sauvignon is the Cadillac of red wines, Chardonnay may qualify as the Lincoln of whites. When the so-called Yuppie generation suddenly got into white wine in a big way, Chardonnay was the wine for creating the proper impression. Hopefully, many who drank Chardonnay for the sake of impression realized this varietal can be an excellent wine. The offerings of respected winemakers can put a sizeable dent in your wallet, just as Cabernet can.

Whereas some Cabernets will knock your socks off with their big taste, Chardonnay's taste is more subtle. However, it can be every bit as complex as Cabernet. It will not complement your steak but is likely to enhance your shellfish extravaganza or stand up to your chicken entrees.

For a while, it seemed as though the arbitrators of society had decided that all one needed to know about wines was that you ordered Cabernet if you wanted red and Chardonnay if you preferred white wine. If you stick with those limits, you'll miss **A LOT!** Nevertheless, an exquisite Chardonnay is an experience not soon forgotten.

SAUVIGNON BLANC or FUMÉ BLANC

Grape: Sauvignon Blanc
Color: Light straw to pale green
Cost: Moderate to expensive
Aging: One of a very few whites that will improve with one to three years of aging.
Foods: Seafood, poultry.
Dryness: Dry to very dry.

Sauvignon Blanc is also marketed as Fumé Blanc. To characterize Sauvignon Blanc as a poor man's Chardonnay is to do this sophisticated wine a disservice. It is a white wine that can have nearly as much character as Chardonnay, but will not cause you to wonder if you need a second mortgage to finance its purchase. Sauvignon Blanc may also improve with aging, as does Chardonnay.

I personally characterize Sauvignon Blanc as having a herbal taste. It can be a complex wine so don't try it with something that requires you to buy your spices by the pound. However, Sauvignon Blanc can serve as a wonderful complement to many delicately flavored dishes and yet stand up to others with stronger tastes.

GEWURZTRAMINER

Grape: Gewurztraminer
Color: Straw green
Cost: Inexpensive
Aging: Drink now.
Foods: Drink by itself, or fish in rich sauces, pork chops, smoked meats, fruit.
Dryness: Semi-sweet.

Gewurztraminer is a white wine that you will never be complacent about. It can taste like someone accidently spilled the spice rack in the bottle, and by the same token, it can be perfect for certain dishes. It is one white wine that can stand up to brawny food or even complement desserts. It is probably the only wine that can complement chinese food. Gewurz can also be a truly great wine to sip out by the pool with slices of cheese and fruit.

This is not a wine that you will find by the carload at your local supermarket. Not many wineries produce Gewurztraminer. But if you find it, it's definitely a wine worth trying. As one guide put it, Gewurztraminer has more personality than almost any other white wine.

CHENIN BLANC

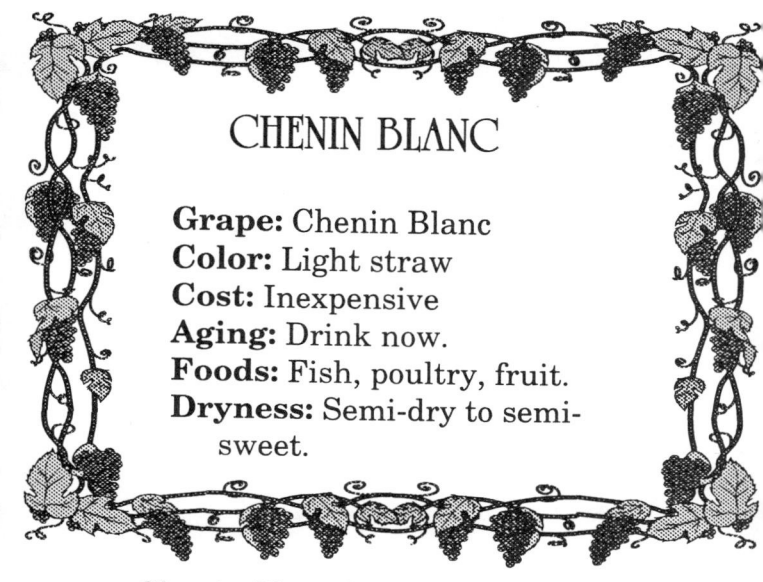

Grape: Chenin Blanc
Color: Light straw
Cost: Inexpensive
Aging: Drink now.
Foods: Fish, poultry, fruit.
Dryness: Semi-dry to semi-sweet.

Chenin Blanc has introduced many wine drinkers to varietal wine. Unlike Chardonnay, it is not a pretentious wine. It may improve for a year or two, but most can be drunk as soon as you get home from the local wine merchant, if it has been stored at a proper temperature. It doesn't cost an arm and a leg, and it goes nicely with a variety of dishes.

Many Chenin Blancs have a touch of residual sweetness that also attracts new wine drinkers who are still wary of **dry** wines. In fact, much of the Chablis* produced in the United States uses varying amounts of Chenin Blanc. If your experience in buying wine has been limited to jug whites, Chenin Blanc may be just the wine to introduce you to the pleasures of varietal wines.

Chenin Blanc is a wine that doesn't vary a great deal from vintage to vintage. Accordingly, when you buy a particular winery's Chenin Blanc, it tends to be dependable from year to year. Of course, even Chenin Blancs offer surprises now and again. That's why wine offers such intrigue.

* Chablis: a generic wine in the United States; a mixture of several varietals. In France, Chablis is an honored wine locality and wine type. More on generics later.

Chenin Blanc usually goes well with poultry and white meat. It can also be a nice wine to serve as part of the appetizer course for your meals.

JOHANNESBURG RIESLING

Grape: Riesling
Color: Golden
Cost: Moderate
Aging: Drink now.
Foods: Drink by itself, or lightly seasoned poultry or fish.
Dryness: Semi-sweet to semi-dry.

Most Johannesburg Riesling's will not test your pucker power. In the United States, they tend to be made in a medium sweet fashion. Some, made as dessert wines, are sweet enough to be the dessert course themselves. And in that setting, they are luscious.

Rieslings are one of the better "stand alone" wines, which means that when your guests arrive, it is a nice wine to either begin or end the evening. Some Rieslings are quite dry and as such serve as complements for your seafood, poultry and even veal dishes.

Riesling is a grape that benefits from remaining on the vine until a mold, "Botrytis cinerea", concentrates the sugar and glycerine content of the grape. The mold is called the "noble rot", which at first brush is certain to make you run the other way. **However,** when botrytis affected grapes are used to make wine, the results are like the honey of the gods. These are the ultimate in dessert wines, and you pay for the privilege. Botrytis doesn't occur every year, which means that when it does, the grapes are all the more prized. Even then, the skills of a winemaker are put to the test handling the grapes, because they will not ferment with the ease of unaffected grapes.

WHITE ZINFANDEL

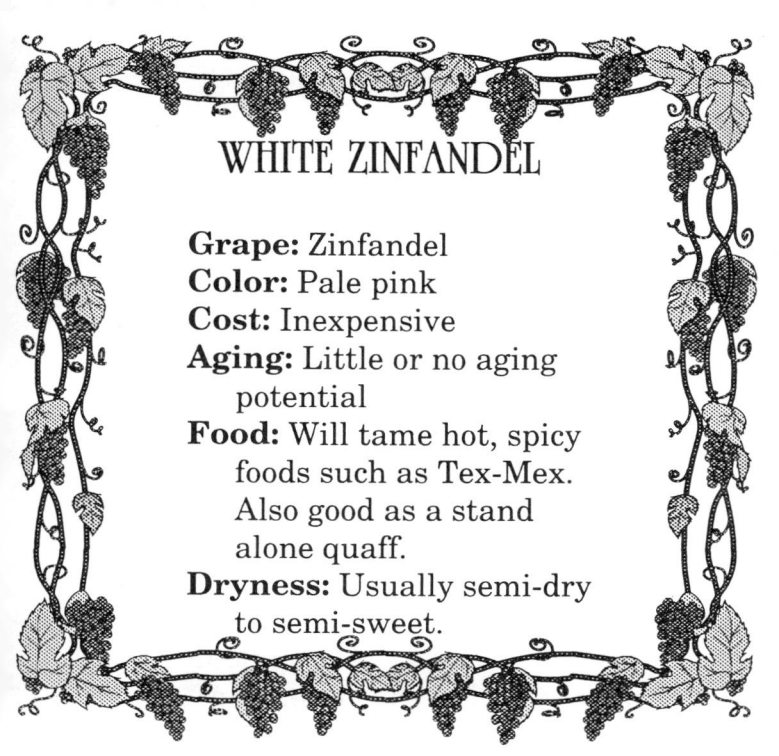

Grape: Zinfandel
Color: Pale pink
Cost: Inexpensive
Aging: Little or no aging potential
Food: Will tame hot, spicy foods such as Tex-Mex. Also good as a stand alone quaff.
Dryness: Usually semi-dry to semi-sweet.

White Zinfandel was developed by removing the skin from the Zinfandel grape early in the crushing and fermentation process. Since the majority of a red wine's color comes from the skin of the grape, the result was a blush wine, or a wine that had just a blush of the original color and quite different taste characteristics. For a time, White Zinfandel was mother's milk to self appointed Yuppies. Fortunately, Yuppies and others discovered they liked White Zin regardless of the social status conferred. Winemakers have jumped to meet this new market and the production of Zinfandel grapes has grown as a result. There are a few wineries that went from being small regional producers to major market forces on the basis of their White Zinfandel production.

Blush wines are also produced from Pinot Noir, Cabernet Sauvignon and other red grapes. Some wineries call the wines they produce by this process Rosé wines while others refer to them as Blush wines. Depending on the grape or grapes used, they can be quite similar or very different. Most can be served with a variety of fish and poultry dishes.

GENERIC WINES

Americans are probably too obsessed with varietal wines for their own good. The French produce quality wines, but designate their wines by the district in which the grapes were grown and blend different varietals together with greater frequency than Americans. French wine drinkers don't appear to suffer. But since the premier products of American wineries are varietal wines, I chose to emphasize the varietal wines commonly available on the shelves of your friendly liquor store or supermarket.

However, unless your name is Megabucks or perhaps Trump, you can't afford to spend a bundle every evening for wine to enhance your dining. Accordingly, it's time you were introduced to *Jug Wine*. Generic wines are usually blends of two or more varietals, frequently bottled in 1.5 and 3 liter bottles (referred to as jug wines), and designed for every day drinking. They are also priced so that you don't have to place large sell orders with your stockbroker before buying.

The most straightforward labeling of generic wines is by color. Thus it is not uncommon in the wine section to see jug wine labeled "Proprietor's Red" or "Uncommonly Good White". Such wines are exactly what they purport to be: a blend of red wine grapes or a blend of white wine grapes.

Just as frequently you will see bottles labeled "Chablis", "Rosé" or "Burgundy". These are **not** varietal wines. Chablis is a blend of white wine grapes and Burgundy is a blend of red wine grapes. They are patterned after French wines bottled in the ancient wine regions of Chablis and Burgundy. Rosé is a generic blush wine made from red wine grapes in the same style as White Zinfandel.

Sometimes a generic wine will contain enough of one varietal (usually 75%) that it could have been sold as a varietal wine. The winery may have good reasons for not doing so. One California winery put out a jug red for several years that was at least 75% Cabernet Sauvignon, and could have been so labeled. But the winemaker's varietal Cabernet had an outstanding reputation, and undoubtedly, the Cabernet grapes going into his jug wine were not of the same quality as what he put into his $50 per bottle varietal wine. Being a shrewd businessman, he didn't want to bring down the reputation of his outstanding Cabernets. And he could always let it be known, which he did, that when you bought his jug wine, you were getting very serviceable Cabernet. It was a win - win situation for him and for those who bought the jug red.

Generic wines would seem to be more of a test of a vintner's skill than varietals because the vintner has to know which wines to blend together to get the effect he wants. If it is a lousy year for Pinot Chardonnay, all the skill, effort and finesse in the world will not turn poor grapes into outstanding wine. But, a winemaker who blends Pinot Chardonnay with Pinot Franc and a touch of Semillion to create a rewarding and serviceable wine has demonstrated genuine skill. It's all the more surprising to me that an outstanding Chablis will never get the recognition that a varietal

Chardonnay will receive. And the winery will never get the same price. I suspect it's for this reason that many wineries have introduced jug varietals (see section immediately following).

By and large, generic wines are not going to be written up in the wine guides. They won't receive rave reviews in the daily press. But by the same token, they will leave you with more than a few coins as change from a twenty when you buy them. They are ordinary wines for daily drinking. Similarly, the grapes used in generic wines are not from that little vineyard perched on the slopes of Howell's Mountain earning the adulation of wine drinkers from all over the world. They are more likely to be from miles and miles of grapes grown near Lodi, California in the central valley and were probably delivered to the winery in railroad tank cars.

Generic wines are drink now wines. They won't benefit from aging. And you don't want to take up the precious room in your wine cellar with a stack of $3.99 jugs of Burgundy (even if it is labeled "Vintner's Select!"). Although most of the better jug wines are corked, screwtop jug wines are perfectly acceptable. (If you aren't going to serve it to J. Arthur Megabucks or perhaps Donald Trump, you don't really care if it's corked, now do you?)

Because jug wine producers buy their grapes in train-load lots and pay close attention to price, one batch of a producer's jug wine may not always taste like the previous batch. This can be a bit disconcerting when you think you've found a jug wine that should be the elixir of the gods, only to discover that the next bottle you buy tastes like it was blended with skunk oil. (Usually, the differences aren't that dramatic, but they can certainly be noticeable.) Some big wineries strive to keep their generic wines consistent through careful attention to blending. Other smaller producers don't have the unlimited access to grapes that the big wineries have, and may have more variation from one bottling to the next. If nothing else, it adds interest to your jug wine drinking. It also means that you can shop the specials on jug wines without going too far out on a limb.

At some point, I hope you will experience an evening when a specially aged Cabernet Sauvignon perfectly matches a roasted leg of lamb. But unless the United States mint provides you with weekly samples of their $100 bills, the wine you'll drink on most occasions will be a generic jug wine. Don't turn you nose up at the Chablis and Burgundy on the supermarket counter. They can enhance many a pleasant evening when the main course is a simple pasta or even a hamburger.

If you opened a 1.5 liter jug and did not finish it, you probably noticed the wine had not improved the next time you tried it. In fact, you may have thumbed through your copy of this book to find the section on "Over The Hill" wines, wondering what you did wrong. Long exposure to air will deteriorate you wine, and even though you hammered the cork in (probably so it wouldn't leak out when you put the bottle on its side in your overcrowded refrigerator), more than half the contents of the bottle may be air. The best way to store remaining wine is to decant it to a smaller bottle. This reduces the amount of air in contact with the wine, and increases its chances for storage without deterioration. Once you've opened a bottle, however, don't count on keeping the remains for weeks after.

Many jug wines are pasteurized before bottling. These wines will not spoil as quickly after opening. The trade off is that they have zero potential for aging. Since most jug wine is bought to be used soon, this need not be a reason to discriminate against pasteurized jug wine. Even pasteurized wine will not keep for months on end. If you only drink wine once or twice a month, you would be better served to buy smaller bottles (such as the four-pack 375 ml bottles now appearing on the market).

Decanting is also used on older bottles of red wine for a different purpose. Red wines often "throw" sediment while aging, which means the last glass may turn out to have small dark particles floating in it. Definitely not the way to impress your boss when you're planning on asking for a raise. In this case, slowly pouring the wine into a decanter or another bottle allows you to leave the sediment in the original bottle instead of in someone's glass.

If you really want to impress people, hold the bottle in front of a candle as you slowly pour, so as to better see the sediment - and to know when to stop pouring.

VARIETAL JUG WINE

Varietal wine is usually bottled in 750 milliliter bottles. In recent years, however, a number of wineries have taken to producing inexpensive 1.5 liter "jug" varietal wines. These contain at least 75% of their wine from one varietal such as Cabernet Sauvignon as opposed to being blends as in generics. I've wondered if wine producers haven't attempted to cash in on our fetish for varietal wines in America. If so, it's too bad. A poor or indifferent wine made exclusively from Cabernet Sauvignon grapes is still a poor or indifferent wine. There are many good 1.5 liter bottles of varietal wine on the market, but in my experience, the majority are seldom as good as the quality varietal wines bottled in 750 ml. bottles.

In dealing with jug varietals, you need to be aware of the difference between wines bottled to compete against jug generic wines and quality varietal wines in larger bottles for customer convenience. While most wine down through the ages has been bottled in a size similar to the 750 ml. bottle, wineries occasionally would bottle their fine wine in larger bottles. Even today, fine wines are occasionally offered in 1.5 liter bottles and even larger sizes, but they are usually separated from the jug wine by your knowledgeable wine merchant.

Inexpensive varietal "jugs" can find service at your table in exactly the same fashion as generic wines.

They will probably not satisfy a wine snob's demand for varietal consistency (Wine labeled Chardonnay should taste like Chardonnay.). However, they can serve as everyday drinking wines as long as they are not harsh or at the other extreme, insipid.

CHAMPAGNE OR SPARKLING WINE

Champagne technically and correctly is a sparkling wine produced only in a specific area within France, known of course as Champagne. While most of us think of all bubbly stuff as "Champagne", most of what is uncorked with that characteristic "pop" at weddings is actually sparkling wine. At least so the vintners in the Champagne region of France (or their lawyers) tell us.

Sparkling wine starts out from some of the same grapes used in varietal wines. However, Champagne and its close cousin, sparkling wine, is processed differently than regular red or white wines (referred to as "still" wines). With sparkling wine, the bubbles come from fermentation in a bottle or closed container that does not let the gas escape and forces it back into solution. When still wines are fermented, the gas is permitted to escape which is why wineries are such pungent places after the crush. Better producers may produce sparkling wines ranging in sugar content from bone dry to stuff that comes close to substituting for the syrup on your pancakes.

True Champagnes from France can cost a bundle. The truly expensive stuff brings visions of waist-coated captains of industry laying aside their Havana cigars and murmuring to the wine steward that a bottle of Verve Cliquot 1935 Brut would top off the evening nicely. Some sparkling wines can also command top prices. Others can be found on the bargain shelves of your local supermarket or wine purveyor and in just about every price range in between. Lot's of cheap stuff is produced every year to lubricate the wedding guests, the folks dedicating new buildings, announcements of new products and on and on. Some of it is little more than bottled headache. Yet, like jug wine, there are many acceptable inexpensive sparkling wines on the market.

STORING YOUR WINE

The ideal place to store wine would be a cave with an ambient year around temperature of 55 degrees. When wine lovers talk about wine cellars, they aren't kidding. A cellar that maintained close to that same temperature would also be ideal. Unfortunately, I happen to live in Phoenix, Arizona where the summer temperature actually hit 122 a couple of years ago, and where cellars are not overly abundant and caves nonexistent (at least on my property). I don't even have an old bomb shelter that I can convert to wine storage. You may not have to cope with summers that make hell seem like a resort, but the likelihood of your having a spare cave or a cellar that runs a dank 55 degrees is unlikely. So what now?

You can:

a) buy aged wine from your local wine merchant, which will cost you;

b) forget aged wine and stay with drink now offerings, which means missing out on half the fun; or

c) you can look into options that won't force you to hock the family jewels.

If you choose option (a), be sure your wine merchant is experienced in handling fine wine. If you usually buy your wine from a drive-through beer warehouse, I'd suggest another approach.

If you choose (c), keep in mind the most adverse condition for wines is rapidly changing temperatures. Wines won't age as well nor keep as long if they are stored in a place that runs a consistent 75 degrees, but they'll be better off than in a place where the temperature swings on a daily basis from 45 to 90 degrees. A dark place is superior to a spot in the sunlight (even reflected sunlight). Light will eventually have an adverse effect on wines, particularly white wines. If you are lucky enough to have an unfinished cellar, it may prove ideal for storing wine, as well as give you the ideal excuse for not putting the effort into converting it into a bedroom for the in-laws. Other options include finished basements (if the in-laws have moved to the Virgin Islands, convert the bedroom to a tasting room!), places in the house that are not heated or cooled, crawl spaces or whatever. Be sure the area doesn't flood in a heavy rain. (I forgot that rule at one place we lived and although our wine wasn't ruined, the labels were sure ugly.)

Other than digging your own wine cellar, the most expensive way to store wine is to buy a professionally built wine cooler. For the mere expenditure of a grand or two, you can buy coolers that will keep up to 100 bottles or more at a perfect 50 to 60 degrees. They look good too if you believe the advertisements. You could probably put them right in your dining room and they'd add to the elegance.

My Phoenix tactic would never meet the approval of the energy conservation folks, but it works. I bought an old refrigerator, set it between the highest possible setting and defrost and the thing holds fairly constantly in the 50 to 60 degree range. It gets a little humid inside, but so are caves. My wife found it is convenient for storing citrus, nail polish and a few other odds and ends. I also store film in it.

Whatever approach you take (closet, garage, underground potato storage, unused bomb shelters), make sure your bottles are on their side or if you are storing cases, upside down. **The cork must remain moist or the wine will eventually spoil.** They should not be in a place where you constantly have to move the bottles to get at something else. (I make my wife store her grapefruit on top of my wine bottles, since grapefruit doesn't suffer if you move it around a lot.) Wine ages best when it is undisturbed.

How long should you store wine before trying it? That depends totally on the wine. Ask where you buy, unless it's the kind of place where you know more about wine than the staff. In that case, wine guides may help. Many guides in discussing particular vintages will recommend cellaring the wine for a certain period. Wineries will sometimes make their own recommendations on the label. If you can afford to, always buy more than one bottle of a particular wine if you are planning on putting it away. Then you can get one bottle out and try it. If the wine is still rough and tannic, you leave the remainder cellared. If it is smooth and drinkable, move the rest of the bottles of that vintage into your "drink soon" category. If the wine is "over the hill", drink the rest as soon as possible or treat a lot of your friends to a gallon or so of your homemade wine vinegar salad dressing.

After reading all this, you can understand why some elect to leave the storing of wine to their friendly merchant. If you can afford the cost and have an experienced wine purveyor to deal with, you will definitely avoid such catastrophes as cellar floods and expensive partially aged bottles rolling out of not quite level refrigerators onto concrete floors. (The purple stain on cement lasts a long time reminding you of your boo boo.) The wine merchant may also have a better feel for when the wine should be on your table instead of in your cellar, helping avoid the "over the hill' syndrome (See next).

OVER THE HILL WINES

Sooner or later, you'll encounter a wine that smells like overripe plums and tastes yucky. One sure way of running across what I call geriatric wines is to frequent restaurants whose wine list is limited to red, rosé and white and who only get an order for red wine every week or so. They buy their wine in gallon jugs. Because the red doesn't go as quickly as white, it tends to go bad. Yet they keep serving it, even though the stuff smells and tastes like an orchard after the harvest (with a lot of bad fruit rotting on the ground).

Not every bottle you put away is going to taste like the elixir of the gods. Some wines never come together and fifteen years of bottle aging wouldn't remove the roughness of the tannin and oak. Others lose their fruit early on, leaving you with only a hint of what the wine should have tasted like. And occasionally, a bottle will go bad.

Your first hint that a bottle has gone around the bend will come when you open it and the aroma is putrid. Chalk it up to experience, bad cork, poor handling at some point, and open another bottle.

You can protect yourself from geriatric wines if you are careful where you buy the wine you plan on keeping. If your own arrangements for keeping wine are not optimal, keep in mind that wine will age faster at higher temperatures. Therefore if a winery recommends keeping a bottle for five years before drinking, and you are storing at 75 degrees, you might want to sample in three years or even less. Higher temperatures are not, however, the best means of speeding up the process of aging a bottle to perfection. For optimum results, stick with 50 to 60 degree cellaring, or as close to it as possible.

SERVING WINE

Down through the years, wine has been drunk from goatskins to fine crystal and probably everything in between. It is not necessary to have a huge collection of glassware for your wine service unless you happen to be the proprietor of an expensive restaurant or are Chief Executive Officer of J. Arthur Megabucks, Inc. The proper glassware will add to your pleasure, however. What makes a glass proper is not its cost, but its shape. In broad general terms, a glass that tapers inward to an opening at the top that is narrower than the body will concentrate the aroma of white wines. The aroma of red wines tends to be more powerful and as a result, red wine glasses are usually bigger and wider at the mouth than white wine glasses.

The glass should be clear. Remember, part of the enjoyment of wine is its color. (Of course if you just realized the Pinot Noir you plan to serve has a murky, dank look, you may want to reach for your pottery glasses - or for the jar in which you keep your salad dressing ingredients.) Tinted glass will obviously affect the way the wine appears and may end up making your wonderfully aged Cabernet look like used motor oil.

Many restaurants offer wine by the glass. And since they don't want to appear to be cheapskates, they invariably fill the glass nearly to the brim. Unfortunately, this is not the best way to serve wine. If the glass is full, there is no space in which the aroma can concentrate and you lose the bouquet and part of the enjoyment of drinking wine. If you have purchased a bottle at the restaurant, you will note the server seldom fills the glass more than half full (unless your server is much more familiar with coffee mugs than wine). Actually filling the glass only one third full is better. Then when you swirl the wine to help bring out the bouquet, you won't slosh it all over the table cloth - or worse, yourself.

Particularly with red wines, bigger is better when it comes to glasses. You don't need to go to the extreme of serving your red wines in a brandy snifter, but the volume of the glass will definitely add to the development of the bouquet. Even white wines should not be served in tiny glasses.

In spite of the millions of saucer-like plastic champagne glasses that are such a common feature of wedding receptions, the best glass for champagne or sparkling wine is actually tall, tapered and narrow. Part of the enjoyment is in watching the little bubbles and those stubby plastic things don't offer much opportunity for that.

When serving red wines, you may also want to reread the comments on decanting under the section on Generic wines.

TEMPERATURE

Wine is sensitive to temperature. Storing and serving it at a proper temperature will add to your enjoyment. You do not have to hire a testing laboratory to make sure your wine is within three tenths of a degree of the mean temperature of Napa, California on September 10th. Nevertheless, wine does not take well to extremes. For instance, unlike a brew, wine is not a beverage you serve **ICE COLD!** Wine over ice is diluted wine. That was all right for the Romans who stored their wines until the stuff was as thick as molasses. But if you are going to spend a few bucks for a good bottle of wine, it's worth a few minutes to learn the temperature at which the wine will be at its best.

Don't be dismayed. We are talking generalities here. So *in general*, wine tends to be served too cold. A basic rule of thumb is that whites should be served at a cooler temperature than reds. If an ideal cellar temperature is around 55 degrees, then white wines can be served at cellar temperature. Reds need to be slightly warmer.

If your wine is too warm, don't toss it in the freezer! Abrupt temperature changes are death to good wine. The best way to cool wine is to put it in a bowl of ice for fifteen to thirty minutes (depending on how warm it is) before you open it. Or you can put wine in your refrigerator to bring its temperature down, since that's a more gradual process. White wine can be refrigerated for several hours before serving. (If you keep your ice cubes in the fresh vegetable section, better cut down the time.) Red wine may benefit from being popped in for fifteen to thirty minutes or so shortly before you plan to serve it.

The primary reason to serve wine at the right temperature is not to impress anyone else. It's to allow the wine to be at its best when YOU drink it.

AIRING

Some wine will also improve if permitted to "air". This is another of those terms, such as "legs", that require translation. To air wine is to pour it into glasses and swirl it a short time before serving. Not all wines need to air. But some do! In that quaint vocabulary wine affectionados develop, some wine will "open up" if permitted to air. While there are no rigid rules for airing wine, red wines are more likely to benefit from airing than whites, since the off odors are generally a biproduct of aging, and red wines are normally aged longer than whites.

Now admittedly, this sounds like a contradiction to all the advice you were given about wine after it has been opened. If you recall, you were told to decant the wine into smaller bottles because air causes the wine to oxidate and taste like rust! Well actually, over the long haul (a day or so), wine is damaged by air. But initially, air can cause the wine to gain both flavor and nose.

I know. If I had warned you about all these contradictions on page three, you would have returned this book and gone back to beer! Hopefully by now, you're hooked! And even if you NEVER air a bottle of wine, you will not be expelled from that great wine press in the sky.

AND FINALLY, ENJOYING

Earlier, I told you that wine was to be enjoyed. Even in spite of the arcane instructions you've received herein -- and the even more arcane terminology -- the bottom line is enjoyment. There's no sense learning how to uncork a bottle of wine, or what temperature to keep it or serve it if you don't enjoy the final product.

If your goal is to one-up everyone you meet, buy another book that teaches you how to be a wine snob. There are plenty on bookshelves throughout the United States. If, on the other hand, you've waded through all this prose because you think you like wine, I hope the information you've gained will be useful.

To me, wine is like color. I cannot describe a brilliant cobalt blue desert sky in the same way I can talk about the soft pink of an Oleander blossom or the multiple grays of a storm cloud. In the same fashion, I can't tell you I prefer blues to reds or greens to oranges. The fruit of the vine all falls under the heading of wine, but wine can be blunt and assertive like a Syrah or quiet and subtle as a Sauvignon Blanc. I hope you will come to know wine in its many varieties and be enriched by the experience, as I have.

A SHORT PRIMER ON THE HISTORY OF WINE

Don't let the word "history" turn you off. It does help to know a bit about wine. Of course, most people are more interested in drinking wine than learning about other people who enjoyed it. But since the editor said I had to have a certain number of pages in this book, we're including this section on history (as well as a section on Italian architecture, Chinese literature, and ancient Navajo curses.).

If you are really into history, read on. If not, may I recommend a cool bottle of dry Chenin Blanc.

We don't know about Homo Erectus, Homo Habilus, Neanderthal or Cro-Magnon but suspect that if they encountered grapes, they may have figured out the benefits of wine. It probably made the days easier - particularly after a acrimonious encounter with the Mastodon that was supposed to be the evening's dinner.

Greeks and Romans drank wine diluted with water. Doesn't say much for either their wine or their water.

We know the Jews drank wine because the Bible speaks of the danger of putting new wine in old wineskins. (That was a sure way of losing your wine - something akin to dropping the wine bottle today as you are emptying the grocery sacks.) As an aside, we can be grateful someone figured out that glass bottles were better than goat skins in spite of the propensity of glass to break when dropped. Cabernet Goat just wouldn't make it in the modern world.

Medieval monks were patient souls. They let their wine sit around until it became Port.

When Germans weren't drinking beer, they drank wine. Actually, it seems from history that Germans drank almost anything intoxicating when they weren't fighting.

The French on the other hand were more into loving than fighting, except about their wine.

The English had the good sense to never say anything bad about French wine. In fact, they imported quite a lot of it over the years. It was one of the very few subjects the English and French ever agreed on.

The Japanese never understood all the fuss about fermented grape juice. Perhaps they were too busy enjoying the virtues of fermented rice, known as sake.

Native Americans discovered early on that North American grapes were more enjoyable fermented than on the vine. But by the time European settlers quit slaughtering the Indians long enough to learn about the possibilities of Concord and Catawba, French wine merchants had already convinced them that French wine was much superior to that of upper New York state. (For more on this, see discussions of balance of trade, and trade deficits.)

If you still feel the need to learn more about the history of wine, I suggest you settle down with a nice bottle of Johannesburg Riesling, and by the time the bottle is half gone, the urge to study history will be too.

If it is not gone, drink the other half of the bottle, go to bed and by the next morning, you won't remember what it is you were interested in doing.

IN SUMMARY

I hope you have learned not to be intimidated by wine. No matter how little or how much we know, there is always more to learn. That's part of wine's fascination. The information in this book is intended as a road map or an outline. Bookstores and libraries are full of books that focus on individual areas. If you find your enjoyment of wine is growing, you may wish to increase your knowledge of this wonderful beverage as well.

Meanwhile, if J. Arthur Megabucks didn't hire you - even for the stockroom - and his wife Medusa sent you the bill for their dinners, hopefully you still came out ahead. If nothing else, I trust you learned from this book that you can enjoy wine without hiring a $500 an hour consultant, buying a library of books, or always having to ask someone else to select from the wine list.

Here's to YOUR enjoyment of the fruit of the vine!

WINE NOTES

WINE NOTES

WINE NOTES

WINE NOTES

Order Form

Postal Orders: Bremo Press
P.O. Box 30604,
Phoenix, AZ 85046-0604.

Please send _____ copies of *Wine 101* at $9.95 per copy to:

Name: _____

Company: (If applicable) _____

Address: _____

_____

City: _____

State: _____ **ZIP:** _____ - _____

Sales Tax:
Please add 6.8% for books shipped to Arizona addresses.

Shipping:
Book rate: $1.50 for the first book and 75 cents for each additional book. (Surface shipping may take three to four weeks.)
Priority mail: $3.00 per book.

Order Now! Great for gifts.

Number _____ X $9.95 = _____

Arizona TAX 6.8% = _____

Shipping = _____

TOTAL = _____